HALLC___

JOKES

FOR KIDS

200 Spooktacular Jokes to Keep You Laughing All Halloween!

By

GUS GLIMMER

Thanks for choosing our 'Halloween Jokes For Kids'! We hope it fills your home with spooky giggles and lots of laughs.

If your little ghouls and goblins enjoyed the jokes, we'd love to hear from you! A quick review would be monstrously appreciated. Your feedback helps us keep the fun rolling and reach more families looking for a good laugh.

Once again, thanks for picking our 'Halloween Jokes For Kids'. We can't wait to hear what you and your kids think!

THIS BOOK
BELONGS TO

_ _ _ _ _ _ _ _ _ _ _ _ _ _

_ _ _ _ _ _ _ _ _ _ _ _ _ _

WHY AREN'T THERE MORE FAMOUS SKELETONS?

They're a bunch of no bodies!

IF A WIZARD WAS KNOCKED OUT BY DRACULA IN A FIGHT WHAT WOULD HE BE?

Out for the count!

HOW DO VAMPIRES GET AROUND ON HALLOWEEN?

On blood vessels

WHAT MAKES HONEY AND LIVES IN A GRAVEYARD?

A zombee!

DO YOU KNOW WHY SKELETONS ARE SO CALM?

Because nothing gets under their skin.

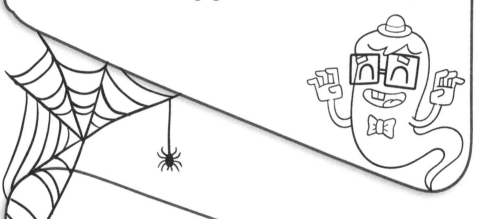

HOW DO YOU KNOW YOUR DOCTOR IS A VAMPIRE?

He draws your blood from
your neck with a straw!

WHAT IS A GHOSTS FAVORITE SNACK?

Boo berries

WHY DIDN'T THE SKELETON CROSS THE ROAD?

He didn't have the guts!

WHERE DOES DRACULA STAY WHEN HE VISITS NEW YORK?

The Vampire State Building.

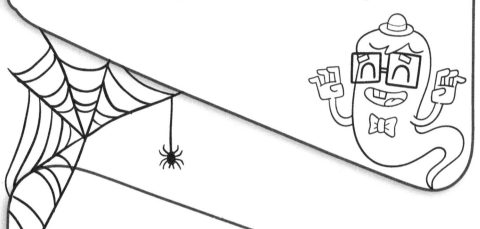

WHAT DO YOU CALL A MONSTER WHO LOVES TO DANCE?

The boogieman!

WHAT DOES A SKELETON SAY WHEN HE WANTS TO EAT?

Bone appetit!

WHAT'S A ZOMBIE'S FAVORITE EXERCISE?

Deadlifts!

WHY DID THE VAMPIRE BRUSH HIS TEETH?

He had bat breath!

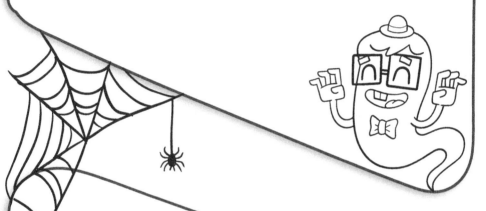

WHAT DO YOU CALL WINNIE THE POOH ON HALLOWEEN?

Winnie the Boo!

ON WHAT DAY ARE GHOSTS MOST SCARY?

Fright-day!

WHAT KIND OF CAR DOES FRANKENSTEIN DRIVE?

Monster truck!

WHAT'S A GHOST'S FAVORITE THING TO READ?

Boo-ks!

WHAT'S A VAMPIRE'SFAVOURITE ICE CREAM FLAVOUR?

Veinilla!

WHAT DO SKELETONS SERVE AT DINNER PARTIES?

Spare ribs!

WHO HAS THE MOST DANGEROUS JOB IN TRANSYLVANIA?

Dracula's dentist.

CAN YOU REPEAT THIS SENTENCE 3 TIMES WITHOUT STAMMERING?

3 witches watch 3 Swatch watches; which witch watches which Swatch watches?

WHAT DO YOU CALL A SKELETON IN THE CLOSET?

Last year's hide and seek champion.

WHAT DO MUMMIES LIKE LISTENING TO ON HALLOWEEN?

Wrap music!

WHAT DO YOU CALL A SNOWMAN IN A GRAVEYARD?

Chilling!

WHAT DOES A PANDA GHOST EAT?

Bam-boo!

WHERE DO GHOST'S BUY THEIR FOOD?

At the ghostery store?

WHO DID FRANKENSTEIN TAKE TO THE HALLOWEEN PARTY?

His Ghoulfriend!

WHY DID THREE WITCHES CALL IN THE PLUMBER?

Hubble, bubble, toilet trouble!

WHAT DO YOU CALL A WITCH WITH CHICKENPOX?

An itchy witchy!

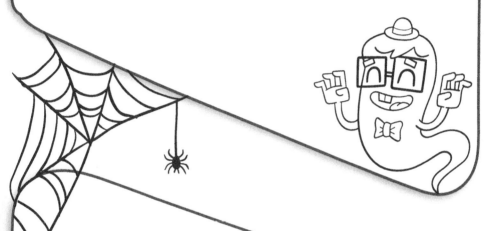

WHY WAS THE PHARAOH SAD?

He missed his mummy!

WHAT DO WITCHES PUT ON TO GO TRICK OR TREATING?

Mas-scare-a

HOW DOES FRANKENSTEIN LIKE HIS EGGS?

Terri-fried!

WHY DO SKELETONS MAKE TERRIBLE DOCTORS?

They don't have the stomach for it!

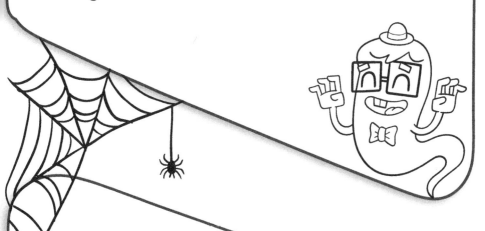

WHAT DO GHOSTS USE TO WASH THEIR HAIR?

Sham-BOO!

WHAT KIND OF DOG DOES A VAMPIRE HAVE?

A bloodhound!

WHAT DO YOU DO WHEN 50 ZOMBIES SURROUND YOUR HOUSE?

Hope it's Halloween!

WHAT SHOULD YOU SAY iF YOU MEET A GHOST?

"How do you boo?"

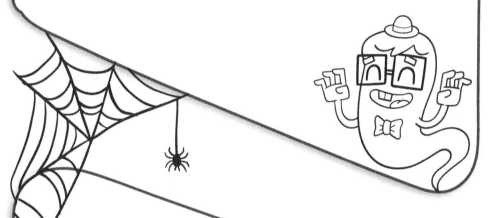

HOW DO YOU MAKE A WITCH ITCH?

Take away the 'w'!

WHAT DO YOU FIND UP A GHOST'S NOSE?

Boogers!

WHAT'S WHITE, SPOOKY, AND HAS EIGHT WHEELS?

A ghost on roller skates!

WHY DIDN'T THE SKELETON GO TRICK OR TREATING

Because he had no body to go with!

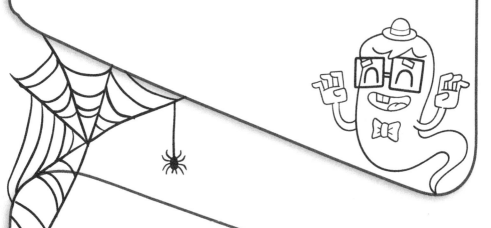

WHAT DOES TWEETY BIRD SAY ON HALLOWEEN?

Twick or Tweet

WHY ARE VAMPIRES UNPOPULAR?

They're a pain in the neck!

WE ALL KNOW ALBERT EINSTEIN WAS A GENIUS...

But his brother Frank was a monster!

WHAT ARE GHOSTS' FAVOURITE TREES?

Ceme-trees!

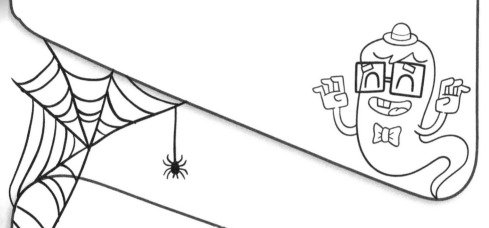

WHAT'S A ZOMBIES FAVOURITE BEAN?

A human bean!

KNOCK, KNOCK

Who's there?
Jack.
Jack who?
Jack-o'-Lantern!

KNOCK, KNOCK

Who's there?
Ivana.
Ivana who?
Ivana suck your blood!

KNOCK, KNOCK

Who's there?
Frank.
Frank who?
Frankenstein!

KNOCK, KNOCK

Who's there?
Boo.
Boo who?
Don't cry! I didn't mean
to scare you.

WHAT'S A ZOMBIE'S FAVORITE DESSERT?

Eyes cream!

WHAT DO YOU GET IF YOU CROSS A TEACHER WITH A VAMPIRE?

A blood test!

WHAT DID THE MONSTER EAT AFTER IT HAD ITS TEETH TAKEN OUT?

The dentist!

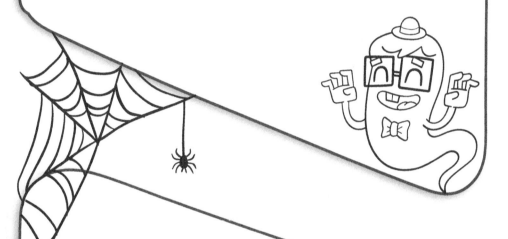

WHAT MONSTER FITS ON THE END OF YOUR FINGER?

The bogeyman!

WHAT DO YOU LEARN AT WITCH SCHOOL?

Spelling!

WHAT KIND OF MISTAKES DO GHOSTS MAKE?

Boo-boos!

WHAT DID THE ZOMBIE SAY TO THE VILLAGER?

Nice to eat you!

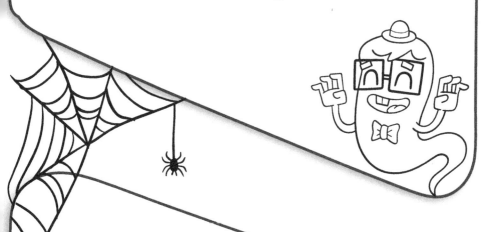

WHAT DO YOU GET WHEN YOU CROSS A SNOWMAN WITH A VAMPIRE?

Frostbite!

WHAT DO ZOMBIES EAT FOR DESSERT?

Ladyfingers

WHERE'S THE ONE PLACE YOU WON'T FIND WEREWOLVES?

The flea market

WHERE DO BABY MONSTERS GO WHEN THEIR PARENTS ARE AT WORK?

Day-scare

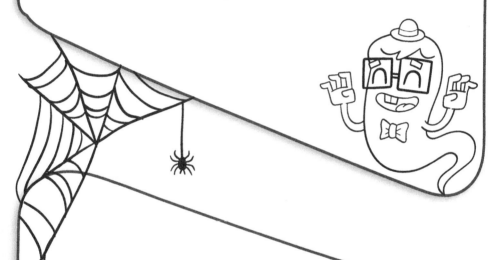

DID YOU HEAR ABOUT THE INVISIBLE MAN WHO WENT TO THE DOCTOR?

He's still waiting to be seen

Who's there?

Wooden shoe.

Wooden shoe who?

Wooden shoe like to give me some Halloween candy?

Who's there?

Fangs.

Fangs who?

Fangs for letting me in!

KNOCK, KNOCK

Who's there?

Voodoo.

Voodoo who?

Voodoo you think you are!

KNOCK, KNOCK

Who's there?

Witch.

Witch who?

Witch way to the haunted house?

WHY WAS THE WITCH LATE FOR WORK?

She over-swept

HOW DO FRENCH SKELETONS GREET EACH OTHER?

They say "bone-jour!"

WHAT'S A VAMPiRE'S FAVORiTE FRUiT?

Neck-tarine

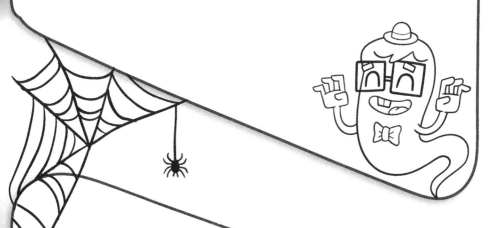

WHO WON THE SKELETON BEAUTY CONTEST?

No body

DID YOU HEAR ABOUT THE GLOOMY JACK-O'-LANTERN?

It needed to lighten up

WHERE DO SPIDERS DO THEIR HALLOWEEN SHOPPING?

On the web

WHAT'S A GHOST'S FAVORITE DESSERT?

Ice scream sandwich

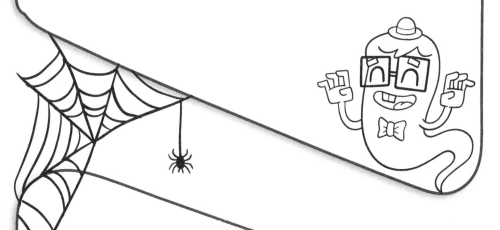

WHAT DID ONE GHOST SAY TO HIS GIRLFRIEND?

"You look boo-tiful tonight!"

WHAT'S A VAMPIRE'S LEAST FAVORITE FOOD?

Steaks!

WHAT DO BATS DO IN THEIR FREE TIME?

Hang out.

WHAT KIND OF SHOES DO GHOSTS WEAR IN THE WINTER?

Boo-ts.

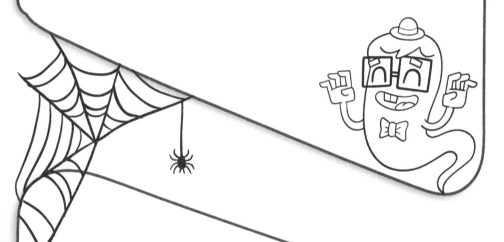

WHAT'S THE BEST THING TO GIVE A SEASICK MONSTER?

Plenty of room!

WHAT KIND OF STREETS DO ZOMBIES PREFER?

Dead ends!

WHY DO ZOMBIES NEVER EAT COMEDIANS?

They taste funny!

WHAT DID THE ZOMBIE MOM SAY WHEN HER GHOULS ASKED TO TAKE THE CAR?

Over my dead body.

WHAT DO YOU GET WHEN YOU DROP A PUMPKIN?

Squash!

WHAT'S A VAMPIRE'S FAVORITE FRUIT?

Blood oranges!

WHAT KIND OF GHOST HAS THE BEST HEARING?

The eeriest!

WHAT SORT OF BIRTHDAY FOOD DO GHOSTS PREFER?

I scream cake!

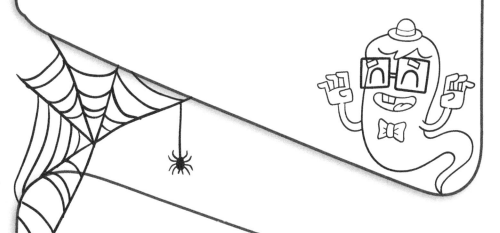

WHAT KIND OF ROCKS DO GHOSTS COLLECT?

Tombstones.

HOW CAN YOU TELL A VAMPIRE HAS A COLD?

He starts coffin

IS THAT A SEED FALLING OUT OF THE JACK-O'-LANTERN'S NOSE?

No, it's snot

WHAT DiD ONE SKELETON SAY TO THE OTHER?

I've got a bone to pick with you

WHY DID THE SCARECROW SKIP DINNER?

He was already so stuffed

HOW CAN YOU TELL A SPIDER iS BORED?

They start climbing the walls

WHY WAS THE JACK-O'-LANTERN SO SAD?

He felt hollow inside

WHAT DO SKELETONS PUT ON THEiR ROAST DiNNERS?

Gravy!

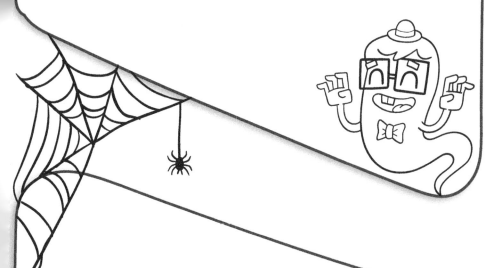

I WENT TO A HALLOWEEN PARTY DRESSED AS A GLOBE AND DIDN'T SPEAK TO ANYONE ALL NIGHT.

I was in a world of my own!

WHY DO HOTEL STAFF DRESS AS WITCHES FOR HALLOWEEN?

Because they provide broom service!

WHY DO VAMPIRES NEVER WEAR MAKE-UP?

Because they can't see their reflection

WHAT DO GHOSTS USE TO PHONE HOME?

A terror-phone.

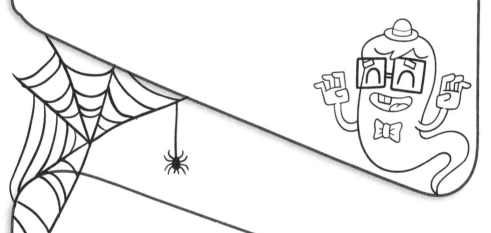

WHAT DO WITCHES PUT IN THEIR HAIR?

Scare-spray!

WHAT'S A SKELETON'S LEAST FAVORITE ROOM IN THE HOUSE?

The living room!

WHAT DO WITCHES PUT ON THEIR BAGELS?

Scream cheese!

WHY DIDN'T THE SKELETON GO TO THE HALLOWEEN PARTY?

His heart wasn't in it!

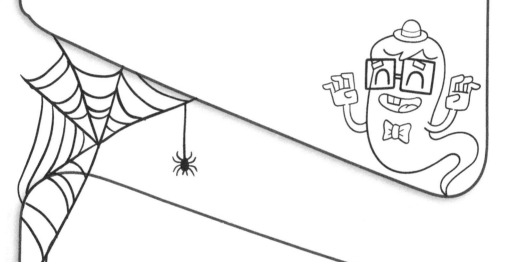

WHAT DOES A VAMPIRE LIKE TO DO IN THE WINTER?

Give frostbites

WHY ARE GHOSTS BAD LIARS?

Because you can see
right through them!

WHERE DO CELEBRITIES GO ON HALLOWEEN?

Mali- boo!

WHY WAS THE SKELETON SO BORED?

He had no body to play with

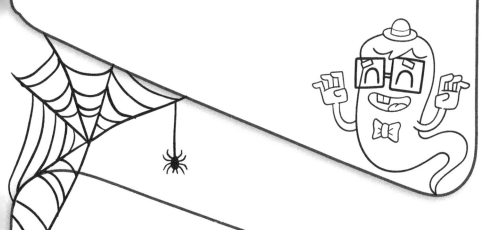

WHERE DO GHOSTS GO FOR A SWIM?

The Dead Sea

WHAT HAPPENS WHEN A GHOST GETS LOST IN THE FOG?

He is mist!

WHAT'S THE PROBLEM WITH TWIN WITCHES?

You never know which witch is which!

WHERE DO VAMPIRES KEEP THEIR MONEY?

At the blood bank

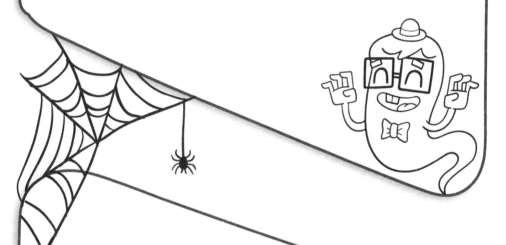

WHAT'S A GHOST'S FAVORITE RIDE AT THE FAIR?

The roller-ghoster!

WHY DO SKELETONS USE SO MUCH LOTION?

Their hands are always bone dry

WHICH HALLOWEEN MONSTER IS GOOD AT MATH?

Count Dracula!

WHAT TYPE OF CANDY SENT THE SKELETON TO THE HOSPITAL?

Jawbreakers

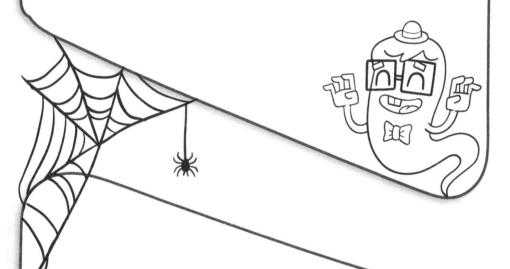

WHY DID THE WITCH GIVE UP FORTUNE-TELLING?

She saw no future in it

WHAT DO YOU CALL A PUMPKIN THAT WORKS AT THE BEACH?

A life gourd

WHAT DO YOU CALL A SPORTY PUMPKIN?

A jock o' lantern

WHAT IS A SKELETON'S FAVORITE KIND OF ART?

Skull-ptures

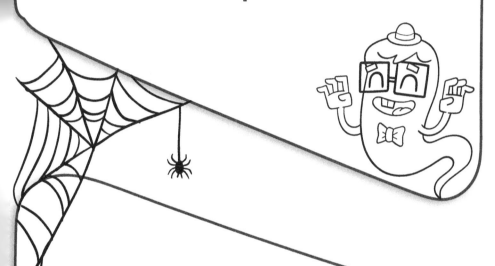

WHAT'S THE BEST WAY TO TALK TO A VAMPIRE?

From very far away!

WHAT DO BABY GHOSTS WEAR ON HALLOWEEN?

Pillowcases!

HOW CAN YOU TELL THAT VAMPIRES LOVE CRICKET?

They turn into bats every night!

WHAT DO YOU CALL TWO WITCHES LIVING TOGETHER?

Broom-mates!

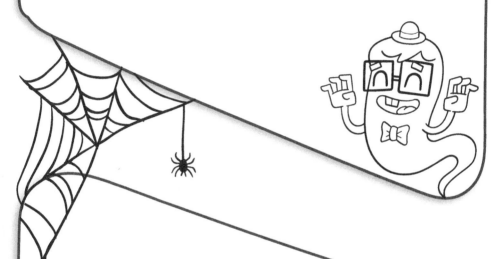

WHAT POSITION DO GHOSTS PLAY IN FOOTBALL?

Ghoul-keeper

WHY CAN'T SKELETONS PLAY CHURCH MUSIC?

Because they have
no organs

WHY DO VAMPIRES NOT WANT TO BECOME INVESTMENT BANKERS?

They hate stakeholders

WHAT'S THE FIRST THING THAT BATS LEARN AT SCHOOL?

The alpha-bat

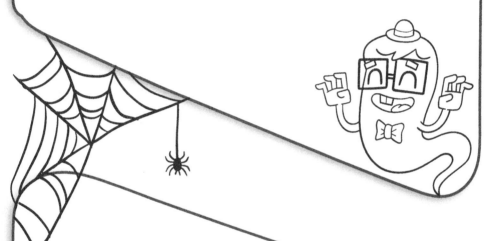

WHY DO BATS LIVE IN CAVES?

Because they rock!

WHAT DID THE SPIDER SAY TO THE FLY?

Buzz off

WHAT SONG DOES DRACULA HATE MOST?

You Are My Sunshine!

WHAT POKÉMON IS DRACULA ALWAYS TRYING TO CATCH?

Koffin'!

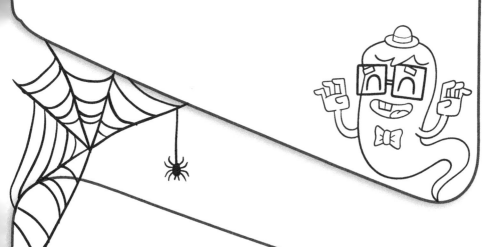

WHAT DOES DRACULA LIKE TO WATCH ON TV?

Neck-flix!

WHAT DiD DRACULA SAY WHEN HE RECEiVED A PRESENT?

Fangs a lot!

WHAT DO YOU CALL DRACULA IF HE'S SHOPPING FOR BARGAINS?

Discount Dracula!

WHAT SPELL DO WITCHES USE WHEN THEY WANT TO CONCENTRATE?

Focus pocus!

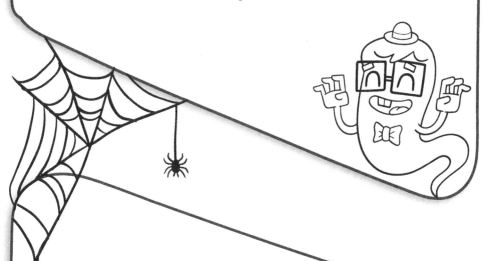

WHAT DO LITTLE MONSTERS CALL THEIR PARENTS?

Mummy and Dead-y!

KNOCK, KNOCK

Who's there?
Olive.
Olive who?
Olive Halloween!

KNOCK, KNOCK

Who's there?
Howl.
Howl who?
Howl-ween is here!

KNOCK, KNOCK

Who's there?

Minnie.

Minnie who?

Minnie people love Halloween.

KNOCK, KNOCK

Who's there?

Creep.

Creep who?

Creep it down, you'll wake the dead.

KNOCK, KNOCK

Who's there?
Ash.
Ash who?
A zombie with a cold.

KNOCK, KNOCK

Who's there?
Gwen.
Gwen who?
Gwen do you think
Halloween will be here?

KNOCK, KNOCK

Who's there?
Bean.
Bean who?
Bean waiting for Halloween all year long.

KNOCK, KNOCK

Who's there?
Phillip!
Phillip who?
Phillip my bag with Halloween candy, please!

WHAT DO GHOSTS DO AT SLEEPOVERS?

They tell scary human stories!

WHAT IS A SKELETON'S FAVOURITE MUSICAL INSTRUMENT?

The trom-bone!

WHAT DO YOU CALL A WEREWOLF THAT USES BAD LANGUAGE?

A swearwolf

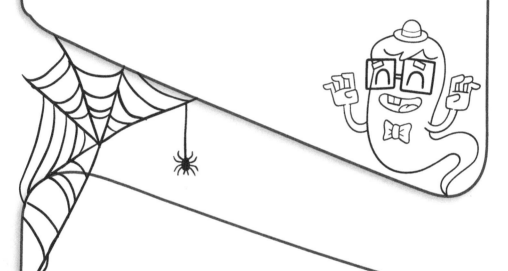

WHO DO VAMPIRES BUY THEIR COOKIES FROM?

The Ghoul Scouts!

WHAT TYPE OF PASTA DO THEY SERVE AT THE HAUNTED HOUSE?

Fettuccine afraido!

WHAT DID THE GHOST TEACHER SAY TO THE CLASS?

Look at the board and
I will go through it again!

WHY DO ZOMBIES NEVER GET LOST?

They always follow their gut!

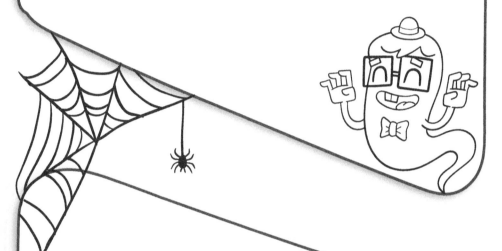

WHY WAS THE JACK-O'-LANTERN SO FORGETFUL?

He was hollow-headed!

WHAT'S A SKELETON'S FAVORITE PLACE TO RELAX?

The bone yard!

WHAT DID THE MUMMY SAY WHEN HE SHOWED UP LATE?

Sorry, I got a little wrapped up!

WHO DID THE SCARY GHOST INVITE TO HIS PARTY?

Any old friend he could dig up!

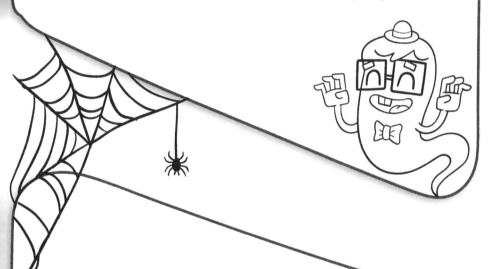

WHAT DO YOU CALL VAMPIRE SIBLINGS?

Blood brothers

WHAT DID ONE GHOST SAY TO THE OTHER?

Get a life!

WHAT DID THE WEREWOLF SAY WHEN HE SAT ON SANDPAPER?

Ruff

WHY ARE GRAVEYARDS SO NOISY?

Because of all the coffin

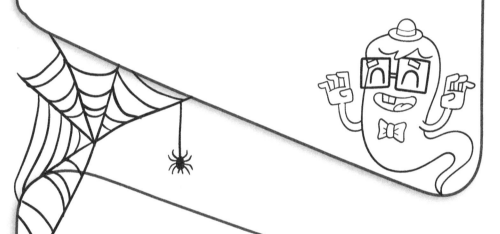

HOW DO YOU FIX A DAMAGED JACK-OLANTERN?

You use a pumpkin patch!

WHAT GOES AROUND A HAUNTED HOUSE AND NEVER STOPS?

A fence

HOW DO YOU MAKE A WEREWOLF STEW?

Keep him waiting

WHAT DID ONE THIRSTY VAMPIRE SAY TO THE OTHER AS THEY WERE PASSING THE MORGUE?

Let's stop in for a cool one!

WHY IS A CEMETERY A GREAT PLACE TO WRITE A STORY?

Because there are so many plots there!

WHY ARE THERE FENCES AROUND CEMETERIES?

Because people are dying to get in

WHY DID THE WEREWOLF GO TO THE DRESSING ROOM WHEN HE SAW THE FULL MOON?

He needed to change

THE MAKER OF THIS PRODUCT DOES NOT WANT IT, THE BUYER DOES NOT USE IT, AND THE USER DOES NOT SEE IT. WHAT IS IT?

A coffin

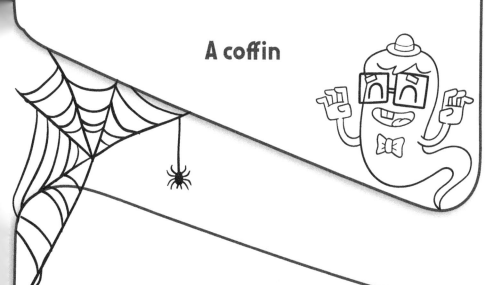

WHAT'S IT CALLED WHEN A ZOMBIES HAS TROUBLE WITH HIS HOUSE?

A grave problem

WHAT IS A RECESS AT A MORTUARY CALLED?

A Coffin Break!

THE SKELETON KNEW WHAT WOULD HAPPEN NEXT

he could just feel it in his bones

WHY DID THE PUMPKIN GO TO JAIL?

It had a bad seed

WHY DID THE ZOMBIE GET FIRED?

It missed the dead-line

DID YOU HEAR ABOUT THE ZOMBIE WHO BOUGHT A NEW CAR?

It cost an arm and a leg

DID YOU HEAR ABOUT THE VAMPIRE FEUD?

There was bad blood

WHAT DO YOU CALL A WEREWOLF WITH A FEVER?

A hot dog

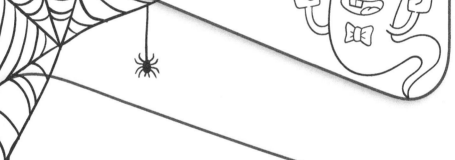

HOW DID THE WITCH SAY GOODBYE TO THE VAMPIRE?

So long sucker

WHAT DID THE WEREWOLF SAY TO THE FLEA?

Stop bugging me

HOW DO VAMPIRE FOOTBALLERS GET THE MUD OFF?

They all get in the bat tub

WHAT DO YOU CALL SOMEONE THAT SUCKS THE JELLY OUT OF DONUTS?

A Jampire

WHY DID THE VAMPIRE BECOME A COMEDIAN LIKE HIS FATHER?

It was in his blood

WHAT DO YOU NAME A DUCK WITH FANGS?

Quackula

WHY DO CYCLOPES GET ALONG SO WELL?

They always see eye to eye

WHAT KIND OF CANDY SHOULD YOU GIVE A TRICK OR TREATING ZOMBIE?

Life Savers

WHAT DID FRANKENSTEIN SAY AFTER BEING STRUCK BY LIGHTNING?

I needed that

WHAT DO YOU CALL A CLEVER MONSTER?

Frank Einstein

WHY DID A SCARECROW WIN THE NOBEL PRIZE?

He was outstanding
in his field

HOW DID COUNT DRACULA START ALL OF HIS LETTERS?

Tomb it may concern

WHAT KIND OF TIE DOES A GHOST WEAR TO A FORMAL PARTY?

A boo-tie

WHAT IS THE FAVORITE PASTIME OF BATS?

Hanging out with friends

WHY DOES FRANKENSTEIN LOVE HALLOWEEN?

He fits right in

WHEN IS IT BAD LUCK TO BE FOLLOWED BY A BLACK CAT?

When you're a mouse

WHAT KIND OF PANTS DO GHOSTS WEAR?

Boo jeans

WHAT IS A BABY GHOST'S FAVORITE GAME TO PLAY ON HALLOWEEN?

Peek-a-boo

WHAT DOES A TURKEY DRESS UP AS FOR HALLOWEEN?

A gobblin'!

WHAT DID THE VAMPIRE SAY TO THE GHOST AT THE HALLOWEEN PARTY?

"Come on! Why don't you live a little?"

WHAT TREAT DO EYE DOCTORS GIVE OUT ON HALLOWEEN?

Candy corneas

WHAT IS A GHOST'S FAVORITE CAR?

A Boo-gatti

WHY DID THE POLICEMAN TICKET THE GHOST ON HALLOWEEN?

It didn't have a
haunting license

WHAT DO YOU CALL A CLEANING SKELETON?

The "grim sweeper"

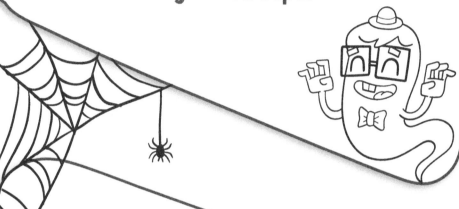

WHERE DOES COUNT DRACULA USUALLY EAT HIS LUNCH?

At the casketeria

WHAT DO YOU DO IF YOU WANT TO LEARN MORE ABOUT DRACULA?

You join his fang club

WHAT CAN YOU SAY ABOUT A HORRIBLE MUMMY JOKE?

It Sphinx!

FANGS FOR READING, LITTLE MONSTER! HAVE A FANG-TASTIC, SPOOK-TACULAR HALLOWEEN FULL OF LAUGHS!

Made in the USA
Monee, IL
29 October 2024